seeking to be christian in race relations

to my wife,

SADIE GRAY MAYS

1.

in the beginning god

Centuries ago a sensitive religious soul looked out upon the universe and the world. He looked at the sun, the moon, and the stars, and they puzzled him. He admired the sky and the land, the sea and the mountain, and these, too, made him wonder. The beast of the field and the forest, the fowl of the air and the earth, the serpent of the land and the water, he both admired and feared. Man was a mystery to him, and woman a creature to be wondered at. In an attempt to explain these marvelous things, he was inspired to say:"In the beginning God created the heavens and the earth."

We shall not argue here over the interpretation of the creation story. We shall not split hairs over its historical accuracy. But I believe that in the sweep of the centuries, no better answer has been given to tell us how the universe and man came to be than the simple expression, "In the beginning God." When we accept all that science has to offer, the riddle of the universe is still unsolved. The universe, the world, and man are mysteries; and the wisest of the wise, including the scientist, reaches a point in his research where, if he is honest, he must say, "I do not wholly understand."

The author of *Genesis* is saying that in the beginning God created the earth. Not man, not blind mechanistic forces, not chance, not natural law, but God created the earth with a purpose for the universe and for man. The Christian church has always declared that the universe and man came from God. It has never accepted the position that man's existence on earth is just an accident nor that the universe is the result of blind chance. It has never taken the position that man is on the earth all dressed up with no place to go. It has always asserted that man's origin is in God and that his eternal destiny is in God.

One may argue as to the "how" and the "why," the "when" and the "where." One may even debate the nature of God, but the Christian faith as found in the Bible and in church creeds reveals no doubt that beyond the universe is God. It has never accepted the view that Nature is able to explain the "nature" of all existence.

Man Is Dependent upon God

What happens to a person after death no one can answer with scientific precision. It is reasonable to argue that there is a close connection between belief in God and some kind of immortality or life beyond the grave. If one does not believe in God, he can hardly believe in a hereafter. He can only believe in immortality through influence or through the lives of one's children. If one believes in God, the God revealed by Jesus Christ, he can easily believe in life after death, whether that life be physical or spiritual. Some believe that life continues beyond this earthly existence; others deny it. Some believe in a heaven and a hell; others do not. Although

preface

It is hardly an exaggeration to say that one of the most disturbing and perhaps the most baffling problem confronting mankind today is the problem of race. Prejudice based on race and color is most difficult to overcome. It is probably easier to be Christian in any other area of life than it is in the area of race. Here the practice of the Christian religion seems to break down most completely.

Race and color prejudice is found in some degree the world over. Though worst in South Africa, and next in the United States, this prejudice is not absent in Europe, Asia, Australia, South America, and other parts of Africa and North America. It operates against the victim in employment, politics, social life, education, and in church and state. Though born without color prejudice, children are indoctrinated with it by their parents at an early age.

In this volume an attempt is made to set down a Christian basis for human relations in the area of race. I have deliberately dealt with what I consider to be a few of the essentials of the Christian faith with a point of view about life for anyone who accepts that faith. If people are called upon to deal fairly with one another and if races are called upon to live together in harmony and justice, there must be a reason. This reason is clearly set forth in the Old and New Testaments.

I believe that in seeking a basis for the elimination of race prejudice and discrimination, we must find such a basis in something other than man. It is not enough for us to call upon members of different races to be decent toward one another for the mere sake of humanity, science, or democracy. The basis for good relations is found in the Christian religion, in the proper understanding of the Christian doctrines of man, Christ, and God, and in the application of Christian insights and convictions in everyday living. Therefore, this book begins with a statement about God.

Although the Universal Declaration of Human Rights of the United Nations, issued several years ago and now revised, lays no claim to being a Christian document, it is definitely Christian in emphasis. The ideas in this pamphlet might well be considered a Christian theological basis for a declaration of human rights. This declaration gives a general background for Christian interracial living and suggests a measuring rod by which Christians of one race may test their daily relationships and attitudes as they mingle with members of any other race.

This volume is intended to present a challenge, not only to the individual Christian, but also to the church, which often divides peoples solely on the basis of race and color.

BENJAMIN E. MAYS

Atlanta, Georgia
November, 1956

contents

seeking to be christian in race relations

by benjamin e. mays

FRIENDSHIP PRESS NEW YORK 1957

Christian people may differ as to the nature of immortality, they generally believe that God does sustain them in this life and beyond death.

What we are most concerned about here is the fact that we are moving into an area over which man has absolutely no control. Science may and does succeed in lengthening man's days upon the earth. How many more years science may be able to add to man's life cannot now be predicted. But no scientist living today has any faith in the idea that man's physical life on the earth can be extended over a period of a million years or even a thousand years.

Call it fate or call it God, man is dependent upon something for the span of his life upon the earth. Somewhere in his earthly existence he comes up against that inevitable event that we call death. He reaches the point where the things upon which he depends for life, such as food, air, sunshine, water, science, wealth, learning, race, nation, and friends no longer sustain him. He dies. And there is nothing he can do about it.

The Christian faith insists that all this is related to the divine purpose and that it is further evidence that man is not self-sustaining; he is dependent upon God. It is useless, therefore, for one to spend time worrying about what will happen to him when he is dead. He has only one thing to worry about, as the subsequent pages will show, and that is: How am I relating my life to God and to man as I go about my task from day to day? And whether he does this well or ill, the consequences of what he does are ultimately in the hands of God. Whether postearthly existence is in a happy place called heaven or a miserable place called hell, whether it terminates in nothing or in a spiritual existence, all of this is beyond the control of man.

Tomorrow's World Is Dependent upon God

The Christian affirms further that man is dependent upon God for the kind of world that he can build. Christianity declares that the universe is essentially ethical and essentially moral. Just as there are scientific and physical laws by which the universe is governed and by which man must abide, there are ethical and moral laws by which man must regulate his life. For example, every high school student is familiar with the simple chemical formula H_2O. He knows that this proportion of hydrogen and oxygen will yield the same result the world over. The chemist discovered the formula, but he did not create the fact that the combination of the proper parts gives us water. Likewise, true friendship between one boy and another produces a happy relationship. Hatred between the two boys leads to estrangement and unhappiness. The fact that love binds two people together and hatred tears them apart is a discovery one may make but not a fact one can create or establish.

Man cannot build the world as he pleases. Many have tried it—the Pharaohs, Cyrus the Great, Nebuchadnezzar, Alexander the Great, the Caesars, Napoleon, Kaiser Wilhelm, Hitler, Mussolini, and many others—but to no avail. God and not man has created the laws that will bring peace among nations. God and not man has created the ethical laws that will guarantee the continued existence of an economic system. Such laws were not created by the exponents of communism, capitalism, nor socialism. God and not man has created the kind of justice that

4

will enable one race to live in harmony with another race. This is not the kind of justice or law that the strong and mighty usually impose upon the weak. It is God's justice. Man's task is to discover God's laws and base his choices and actions upon them.

Contrary to popular opinion, the future of the world is not necessarily in the hands of the nation possessing the largest number of billions in dollars, the nation with the most economic resources, nor even the nation with the most powerful air force and the largest stockpile of thermonuclear weapons. The Christian faith affirms that righteousness and not armaments, justice and not economic power ultimately sustain a nation and that the spiritual laws that make this so are just as real and just as unchangeable as are the laws of science. History proves definitely that a nation can become so corrupt, an economic order so unjust, a race so brutal that all the billions, all the bombs, and all the navies and planes cannot save that nation, economic order, or race. There are forces at work in the universe that are beyond the control of man.

The Scientist Is Dependent upon God

The scientist who may deny his dependence upon God must rely upon a dependable, orderly, trustworthy universe—an orderliness that is there, that he discovers, but that he cannot create. The astronomer who predicts with almost mathematical precision that the next comet will appear fifty, seventy-five, or one hundred years from now and misses it by only a few minutes is depending upon a universe that is orderly and trustworthy. The astronomer and the scientist may call this orderliness natural law, but the Christian calls it God.

The biologist who rejects the creation of man as recorded in *Genesis* and who affirms with certainty that man evolved from simple forms to more complex structures is relying upon an order that is predictable, an order that he discovers but an order that he cannot create. The biologist may call it evolution, but Christian faith attributes this order to God.

In other words, the Christian faith contends that the scientist is dependent upon God. Without a trustworthy, dependable, orderly universe, the scientist could not function. Man does not lie awake at night nor set an alarm clock for a certain hour in order to get up in the morning to hang out the sun. He has faith that the sun will rise.

Man Must Believe in God

Finally, the Christian faith makes it clear that man cannot live without God. It is the nature of man to look beyond himself for help. The quest for God is a search for something upon which one can rely completely. In this sense every person is in search of God. He must either believe in the God of the Christian faith, adopt the god of some other faith, or invent a god of his own. He must be devoted to something beyond himself that is worthy of complete allegiance.

It is not too much to assert that man must either believe in a god or die in despair. When the Communists in Russia made war on Christianity, many people felt that they had abolished God. But it is clear that when they rejected the Christians' God, they adopted a classless society as their god and gave themselves to this idea. They abolished Christ as a symbol of their hopes and adopted instead Karl Marx and his gospel.

The Nazis in Germany, between 1939 and 1945 and earlier, attempted to abolish Christianity. They substituted Adolph Hitler for Christ and looked to him as their savior. They made the German race their god. They went out to fight, to bleed, and to die for Herr Hitler and for German "blood" and soil.

The Fascists in Italy, during the same period, subordinated Christ and God by elevating Benito Mussolini to the role of Christ and the Italian State to the role of God.

The American humanists, at the same time, dethroned God when they accepted in his stead a glorified humanity.

It is clear that man cannot live without some sort of god. He must give allegiance to something beyond himself.

The Christian God Is the God of Every Race

But no belief in God is adequate unless it is a belief in a universal God, who is a God of justice, mercy, and love. He cannot be a racial nor a national god. He cannot be a class god. He must be God for all peoples. The God whom Christians worship is that kind of God—a universal God, a God of every nation, race, and clan. When we lose sight of this fact, only a god of a particular nation, culture, or race is left.

This light broke upon Peter in his experience with Cornelius when he exclaimed:

" 'You yourselves know how unlawful it is for a Jew to associate with or to visit any one of another nation; but God has shown me that I should not call any man common or unclean. . . . Truly I perceive that God shows no partiality, but in every nation any one who fears

him and does what is right is acceptable to him' " *Acts*
10:28, 34-35.

The light broke upon the Apostle Paul when he
smashed the bonds of the law and discovered that God
was a God for all peoples and said:

". . . for in Christ Jesus you are all sons of God,
through faith. For as many of you as were baptized into
Christ have put on Christ. There is neither Jew nor
Greek, there is neither slave nor free, there is neither male
nor female; for you are all one in Christ Jesus" *Galatians*
3:26-28.

The true Christian can believe in no other kind of God.
In his dealing with people, he sees them first as human
beings, children of one God, and second as members of
a particular nation or race. A German is first a human
being, a child of God, and secondarily a German. A
Negro is first and foremost a human being, a child of
God, and incidentally a Negro. A Mexican is a child of
God first and secondarily a citizen of Mexico. Even a
murderer is first a human being, a child of God, and
accidentally a murderer. It is in this order that our treatment of all people must proceed if we are Christians.

2.

the uniqueness of man

The Christian faith as revealed in the Bible makes it clear that man is unique among the creatures of the earth. It is not too much to say that when God reached man in the creative process, he did for man what he did not do for any other creature. The author of *Genesis* tells us that God breathed into man's nostrils his own breath, and man became a living soul. God did not do this for the beasts of the field nor for the fowls of the air nor for the fish of the sea—only for man.

The writer is accounting for the uniqueness of man. He shows clearly that man is "somebody" and that he is important not in his own right, but because God conferred dignity and value upon him. For this reason it is a foolish notion that man has special distinction merely because he belongs to a particular race, nation, or family.

It is also important to note that when referring to creation the author of *Genesis* makes man a unique creature in his declaration that man was created in God's own image. The Christian faith fully comprehends man's unique place in the universe. Centuries before modern science demonstrated man's superior status, the Christian religion had affirmed it.

Science and Religion Agree

Within recent years science has come to the support of the Christian religion in three very important areas:

1. The Christian faith and science agree that man has a common origin. They differ as to what the origin is, how it came about, where and when, but they both stand on common ground in the assertion that the human family began as one. There is not one origin for the white man, another one for the Negro, and another for the Mongoloid. Whether one turns to science or to the Christian faith as revealed in the Bible, the verdict is the same: the various races of mankind the world around have a common ancestry.

2. Science and Christianity also agree that man is different from any other creature that inhabits the earth. From an evolutionary point of view, man stands at the top; from a religious point of view, man stands at the top. Man demonstrates his superiority to the animal by his speech, by his intellect, and by his conscience. There is no distinction as far as racial origin is concerned.

3. The Christian faith and science agree further that all mankind is related. The structure of the body proves kinship. In all normal human beings, we find the same number of toes, fingers, teeth, muscles, and bones. There are tall people and short people in all parts of the world. There are long heads and round heads among all races. There are brilliant people and stupid people in every race of mankind.

Science has demonstrated that there are four types of blood, called O, A, B, and AB. If an examination is made of the blood of an African Negro, an American white man, an Indian American, an Englishman, a Chinese or a Japanese, it will be found that all have one of these four types.

Also people behave pretty much the same way the world around. If we are kind to them, they are likely to respond with kindness. If we insult them, they are likely to turn against us. The human family is one.

From the standpoint of the Christian faith, man has a common father, God. From the point of view of science, man has a common ancestry. It is implicit in the Christian faith that all men are brothers, sons of one father.[1] Science proves that by blood all men are brothers.

If God is a common father and if all men are brothers, then it inevitably follows that the human family is one family. It belongs together. The destiny of each individual wherever he resides on the earth is tied up with the destiny of all men that inhabit the globe. Whether we like it or not, we cannot do anything about it. It is a fact. The English poet and cleric, John Donne, has set the idea in language that is immortal:

> No man is an Iland, intire of it selfe;
> every man is a peece of the Continent,
> a part of the maine;
> if a Clod bee washed away by the Sea,
> Europe is the lesse, as well as if a Promontorie were,
> as well as if a Mannor of thy friends or of thine owne were;
> any mans death diminishes me, because I am involved in Mankinde;

[1]Some Christians take exception here. They hold that God is the creator of all men but that he is the father of believers only. In this case only believers are brothers, but believers belong to all races.

And therefore never send to know for whom the bell tolls;
It tolls for thee.[1]

It is the belief of the Christian that the life of each individual is of supreme worth and value. Man is created in God's image. Therefore, the life and happiness of every human being must be respected.

Either All or None

Science has proved that by blood all races are kin. Christianity believes that God is the common father and that human life is of intrinsic worth. Yet it is not enough for anyone simply to say, "I grant these things." It is too easy to call *all* men brothers and then act as if only *some* men are brothers. We must go further. Either *all* men are brothers or *no* men are brothers. Either God is the father of *all* men or he is the father of *no* men.[2] Either the lives of *all* children are sacred or the life of *no* child is sacred.

If the Americans and the English are brothers, then the Americans and the Russians are brothers. If God is the father of the Chinese, he is the father of the Japanese. If the life of the Queen of England is sacred, then the life of a miner in Wales is sacred. If the life of the President of the United States is of supreme worth, then the life of a mill hand in one of the Carolinas is of supreme worth. If the life of a multimillionaire is precious, then the life of a sharecropper is precious. If the life of a white child

[1]*Devotions upon Emergent Occasions by John Donne,* edited by John Sparrow. Cambridge, Cambridge University Press, 1923, p. 98. Used by permission.

[2]See footnote on preceding page.

comes from God, then the life of the blackest Negro child also comes from God. All have worth. Even the Christian who excludes nonbelievers from God's fatherhood cannot logically deny that among believers there should be no barriers based on race, color, or nationality.

All Human Beings Are Unique

History is filled with examples showing that God has raised up significant persons from every race and land and from every level of society. Although they came from two extremes in the socio-economic world, William Shakespeare and John Milton were among the greatest of poets, Ludwig van Beethoven and George Frederick Handel among the greatest musicians, Abraham Lincoln and Franklin Delano Roosevelt among the greatest presidents of the United States, and Robert G. Menzies and Winston Churchill among the world's greatest leaders. Though from a minority and much persecuted people, our greatest prophets and many of our leading scientists, composers, philosophers, and statesmen were and are Jews. Amos and Hosea, Isaiah and Jeremiah, Ezekiel and Micah were Jews. So were Abraham and Moses, Jesus and Paul. Spinoza the philosopher, Mendelssohn the composer, Einstein the physicist, Freud the psychologist, Disraeli the statesman, Karl Marx the economist, and Brandeis the jurist, all of these were Jews.

Rabindranath Tagore, a Hindu of Bengal, ranks as one of the great poets of modern time. T. Z Koo, Chinese, and Toyohiko Kagawa, Japanese, are among the most widely known Christians of our day. The greatest exponent of the doctrine of nonviolence was Mahatma Gandhi, of India. Negroes are among the most skilled

13

artists of our time. Marian Anderson, Roland Hayes, and Mattiwilda Dobbs have thrilled the world with their songs. Negroes are among the greatest athletes in the world of sports. The names of Joe Louis, Jackie Robinson, and Roy Campanella are at the top in the annals of sports. Some of America's outstanding educators are Negroes, and Negroes stand high as writers, diplomats, scientists, and religious leaders. Booker T. Washington, Mary McLeod Bethune, and Mordecai Johnson will be remembered as outstanding among educators. Ralph Bunche in diplomacy, George Washington Carver in science, and Howard Thurman in religion stand at the front in their respective fields. An appraisal of many areas of American life would show members of racial minorities in positions of leadership. The uniqueness of man cuts across nationality and race. Truly God is not partial.

We quote approvingly the anthropologist, Franz Boas:

"If we were to select the most intelligent, imaginative, energetic, and emotionally stable third of mankind, all races would be represented."

Man Is Unique Because He Is Free

The Christian religion has always declared that man is a free agent because he is never wholly a slave to the conditions in which he finds himself. He can rise above the current practices that go on around him and live a creative, helpful life in the midst of the most crippling circumstances. The Jews and the Samaritans did not love each other, but Jesus did not hate the Samaritans. The English dominated India for decades, but Mahatma Gandhi harbored no ill will against the English. Booker T. Washington was segregated and discriminated against by the South, but he carried no malice in his heart toward Southern white people. Lillian Smith was born, was reared, and lives in the South, but she has no prejudice against Negroes.

So man or woman, boy or girl, can live in a community of hatred and ill will without hating. No person is bound to be prejudiced against Jews, Negroes, or Gentiles just because prejudice against them is deep-seated in his community. Any person, with God's help and grace, can rise above prejudice against any religious or racial group. It is this freedom in man to think, to choose, to see values and to pursue them, and his power to create a better community that helps to distinguish him from the beast.

3.

love of god and love of man—inseparable

The Christian faith as stated in the New Testament affirms that the love of God and the love of man is one love. Few people recognize the fact that Jesus got into trouble not so much because he believed in God but because he believed in the sacred worth of the individual soul. If Jesus had gone throughout the Palestinian or Greco-Roman world merely talking about God and doing nothing to help man, he would hardly have run into trouble because almost everyone in the world of his day believed in God or in gods. Jesus got into trouble because he believed in man, a belief interlaced and interwoven with his concept of God.

Jesus Combined the Two

When Jesus combined, in deeds as well as in words, the two great commandments of the Old Testament—the love of man for God and the love of man for his brother —he was not simply adding one commandment to another commandment and getting two. He was merging into one Great Commandment the love of God and the love of man so that these two commandments became inseparable.

Jesus made a profound remark when he said to the young lawyer: " 'On these two commandments depend all the law and the prophets.' " He was simply saying that when you interpret and summarize all the law and everything the prophets have said, it adds up to one thing: love God and love your fellow man. Let us recall the incident as recorded in *Matthew* 22:35-40:

"And one of them, a lawyer, asked him a question, to test him. 'Teacher, which is the great commandment in the law?' And he said to him, 'You shall love the Lord your God with all your heart, and with all your soul, and with all your mind. This is the great and first commandment. And a second is like it, You shall love your neighbor as yourself. On these two commandments depend all the law and the prophets.' "

God and Neighbor Belong at the Center of Life

It is reasonable to ask: When does man love God with all his heart, soul, and mind? When does he love his neighbor as he loves himself? Who is his neighbor? It is important that everyone should try to clarify these questions for himself.

There can hardly be any doubting the fact that man is ultraselfish and that selfishness is the cardinal sin of mankind whether it finds expression in the nation that wants to be God, in the race that wants special privileges, or in the individual who sees and judges everything according to his own likes or dislikes. A friend of mine is correct when she declares that, by and large, "man loves neither God nor his neighbor but himself." Too often we act as if God is to be served because of the advantage that we may get by serving him and as if friends are necessary because of the popularity they bring to us, the jobs we secure through them, or the flattering compliments that we receive from them.

The conduct that is sinful when observed in others becomes virtuous or forgivable when observed in ourselves. Because we belong to a particular race, we want privileges for ourselves that we stubbornly refuse to grant to members of other races. The Afrikaners are wicked, we say, because of the way they treat the Indians, the colored or mixed people, and the Negroes in South Africa. But "we don't talk about that" when it is pointed out that we are just as wicked because of the way some Americans behave toward certain national, racial, and religious groups—Mexicans, Japanese, Indian Americans, Negroes, Puerto Ricans, and Jews, for example. Some of us deny them jobs, pay them less for the work they do, refuse to give them equal educational and recreational opportunities, deny them respect and friendship, refuse to admit them to hotels and restaurants, threaten and even kill some who attempt to exercise their right to vote. We are all prone to look at life and the world from our own selfish point of view, conditioned by our prejudices and our fears.

When Jesus summed up the law and the prophets by urging man to love God first and his neighbor as himself, he was trying to get man to dethrone himself and put God and his neighbor at the center of his life. When a person, youth or adult, accepts Jesus Christ as his Saviour and Lord, he recognizes this relationship of self to others and to God. Then the relationship that Jesus taught and lived and died for becomes his way of life. When this happens he is a new creature.

We Love God—When?

Man loves God with all his heart, soul, and mind when he recognizes and acts upon the fact that man is limited and that he is dependent upon God who is not limited. Man must depend upon God for the origin of the phyical universe, for human life, for what it takes to sustain life —sunshine and rain, air to breathe, and food to eat. Man must depend upon God for the physical laws by which the universe is governed, for the ethical laws that make social relations happy, for the kind of future that he can work for, for the length of time he can live on the earth, and for what happens to him when he is dead. Whether we like it or not, these are the limitations under which we must all live. If we work within the area of our limitations, love God, and never try to act as God, we shall be happy. If we attempt to be gods, we shall be miserable, and disaster will result.

It is an interesting observation that the author of *Genesis* saw sin entering the world when man became dissatisfied with his limited place and wanted to be God. This point of view is vividly portrayed in *Genesis* 3:2-5:

"And the woman said to the serpent, 'We may eat of the fruit of the trees of the garden; but God said, "You shall not eat of the fruit of the tree which is in the midst of the garden, neither shall you touch it, lest you die." ' But the serpent said to the woman, 'You will not die. For God knows that when you eat of it your eyes will be opened, and you will be like God, knowing good and evil.' "

It might be said that man's pride, his wanting to be what he is not and what he cannot become, is responsible

19

for the sin in the world and for the terrible condition in which man finds himself today. Man is not all powerful. He is not God, and he can never become God. The more potential evil one finds in developing the mind and using its skills for destructive purposes, the more necessary it is that man does not deceive himself into believing that he is monarch of all.

One should feel toward God somewhat as a devoted child feels toward his or her parents. Real love, devotion, and adoration are present. Along with dependence goes a sense of obligation to God for what he is, for what he does, for what he makes possible daily, as well as for his goodness and mercy, for his loving kindness and his constant forgiveness of our sins.

When we recognize our dependence upon God, we worship and serve him not for selfish ends, but because we love him. The motive behind our worship is neither fear of hell nor hope of heaven. We trust God, and we do not expect him to change the nature of the universe in order to make an exception in our case. We accept the fact that we are our best selves and we make the best possible contribution to the world when we seek to fulfill our destiny within the purpose and plan of God as revealed in the life and teachings of Jesus Christ, recorded in the New Testament.

When one does these things, he obeys the first commandment, which is to love God with all his heart, soul, strength, and mind. He loves God with all he has—heart, soul, strength, mind, emotions, and will.

But there is more, a second commandment. We love God when we obey the command, "Love your neighbor as yourself."

Who Is My Neighbor?

Although the good Samaritan did not do the job of a modern social worker and initiate a program to clear the Jericho Road of thieves, the definition Jesus gave for neighbor has stood and will stand the test of time. A certain man on the way to Jericho fell among thieves who robbed him, beat him, and left him half dead. A priest coming down the road crossed to the other side and passed by him. So did a Levite, an assistant to the priest. Then came a Samaritan, a member of a group despised by the Jews, who stopped to help. He dressed the injuries of the wounded man, took him on his own beast to an inn, and left money for his expenses. Jesus declared that this man who showed mercy was a neighbor to the one who fell among thieves, rather than the members of his own group.

In modern speech, this means that neighborliness is not defined in terms of nationality or race. It cannot be defined in terms of geography. A true neighbor is one who responds helpfully and sympathetically to human needs. Those needs may be physical, social, intellectual, or spiritual, but whoever ministers to them is a real neighbor.

It is also implied in the passage that anyone who is in need is a neighbor as well as the one who responds to the need. If this is so, every one who walks the earth is a neighbor to every one who is in need. The wealthy man dying of cancer, the poor man dying of starvation, the penniless youth wanting to go to college, the weak exploited by the strong are all in need, and they are all our neighbors.

Love Your Neighbor As Yourself

Now the other question: When does one love his neighbor as he loves himself? It seems obvious that one loves his neighbor as he loves himself when he is willing to do—and does do—all he can to respond in a helpful way to meet the needs of another.

We love our neighbors as we love ourselves when we do not seek special privileges for ourselves at their expense, when we forgive them for wrongs done to us, when we take the initiative to restore a broken fellowship, and when we make amends for wrongs we have done to another. Indeed, we should want no special favor that we would not willingly grant to our neighbors, whatever their race, class, creed, or national background.

Jesus showed us that love of God is not isolated from man's everyday activities. We can demonstrate our love for God by demonstrating our love for man in definite, concrete ways.

Love of Man Got Jesus into Trouble

When Jesus began to show his love for man, his trouble began. He was called by God to his ministry, sent by him to bring salvation to man, " '. . . to preach good news to the poor . . . . to proclaim release to the captives and recovering of sight to the blind, to set at liberty those who are oppressed' " *Luke* 4:18.

The clashes that Jesus had with the Roman officials, the scribes, the Pharisees, and the Sadducees were mainly clashes in the interest of man. The most scathing criticisms that Jesus ever uttered against his religious colleagues are found in the twenty-third chapter of *Matthew*:

" 'Woe to you, scribes and Pharisees, hypocrites! for you tithe mint and dill and cummin, and have neglected the weightier matters of the law, justice and mercy and faith . . . .' " The controversy here is not about God but about what these religious leaders were doing to men. " 'They bind heavy burdens, hard to bear, and lay them on men's shoulders; but they themselves will not move them with their finger.' " He was defending the rights of the oppressed. " 'Woe to you, scribes and Pharisees, hypocrites! for you traverse sea and land to make a single proselyte, and when he becomes a proselyte, you make him twice as much a child of hell as yourselves.' "

It is clear that here, as elsewhere in his ministry, Jesus was doing what he conceived to be God's will. When he began to behave in obedience to God's command, the Roman officials called him a traitor, the Pharisees denounced him as a heretic, the Sadducees accused him of being a menace to correct procedure, the Zealots looked upon him as an appeaser and a coward, and the members of his own family said he was out of his mind. In an atmosphere like this, those who opposed him never ceased to hunt him and they finally crucified him. His belief in man, which went with his belief in God, is what sent Jesus to the cross.

It is very clear that man's love for God is inseparable from man's love for man. The author of *I John* states it perfectly when he says:

"If any one says, 'I love God,' and hates his brother, he is a liar; for he who does not love his brother whom he has seen, cannot love God whom he has not seen. And this commandment we have from him, that he who loves God should love his brother also."

4.

a god-man-centered religion

One of the great difficulties of life is to avoid extremes. Professor H. Y. Britan of Bates College used to say in his philosophy classes, "Truth is seldom if ever found in extremes." We need to avoid the extremes in religion. We run the risk constantly of making our religion either completely God centered or entirely man centered.

When we make it completely God centered, we commit the fatal blunder of trying to establish connection between ourselves and God without due regard to our neighbor. We seem to think that we can shut our closet door, pray, and make everything right with God, then in our daily lives cheat, hate, exploit, and even kill.

If our religion becomes too God centered, it is likely to become highly otherworldly, a religion whereby we seek mainly to save ourselves from a burning hell or to win a place of heavenly rest after this earthly life has ended. History is full of examples of this kind of religion where the church puts on revivals, calls "sinners" to repentance and seeks to save their souls while the great social evils—poverty, unemployment, slavery, disease, crime, war, racial discrimination, political and economic injustice—go untouched and unchallenged.

When religion becomes almost wholly God centered, we tend to pay God off by worshiping him. We spend much time arguing about the nature of God and the nature of Jesus. We build beautiful churches and construct costly cathedrals where only the "elite" can belong. Or we spend more time raising money for repairs and additions and for clearing the church of debt than we do teaching children and adults about their relationship to God and man. We do all this in the name of God, but we do it with little regard for the social and physical well-being of man.

When our religion becomes wholly man centered, we risk committing the unpardonable sin of making man into a god. We are likely to ignore the existence of the God in whom Jesus believed and the God whom the Christian is supposed to worship. We may deny purpose in the universe, finding it nowhere except in man. The completely man-centered religion is likely to lead man to believe that he is self-sufficient and that he can lift himself entirely by his own bootstraps. His ethics may become a man-centered ethics with no reference beyond itself. Such a religion is self-defeating because man ends up by worshiping himself and glorifying humanity. The completely man-centered religion leads one to believe that social reform is enough, that personal or group worship is unnecessary, and that no time is needed for spiritual growth.

The Perfect Balance Was in Jesus

At this point Jesus was never misled. More God-conscious than any other personality known to history, he combined in his person, life, and religion the perfect relationship between himself and God and between himself and man. The religion of Jesus might be thought of as a triangular religion, and an equilateral triangle at that. The three sides of the triangle for Jesus were God, man, and himself. This was, and still is, a delicate relationship —so delicate that in every move the whole triangle is involved. When for Jesus the God side of the triangle touched upon the self side, the man side of the triangle was automatically involved. Using passages in the New Testament as data, we shall attempt to prove beyond doubt that the position taken here is sound.

In the sixth chapter of *Matthew,* where Jesus is teaching his disciples the Lord's Prayer, he takes it for granted that men are going to forgive one another if they want and expect God to forgive them: " 'And forgive us our debts, as we also have forgiven our debtors.' " Following the prayer, Jesus states clearly that forgiveness on God's part is granted on condition that we ourselves forgive others: " 'For if you forgive men their trespasses, your heavenly Father also will forgive you; but if you do not forgive men their trespasses, neither will your Father forgive your trespasses.' " In this connection there is hardly any doubting the fact that man's good relationship to God is definitely dependent upon and conditioned by man's good relationship to man.

In the eighteenth chapter of *Matthew,* the question of forgiveness is carried still further. There Jesus is trying to show that in good religion one does not seek revenge and that the only thing that breaks the vicious circle of "an eye for an eye and a tooth for a tooth" is forgiveness. He teaches in this chapter that whenever any person trespasses against you, the thing to do is to " 'go and tell him his fault, between you and him alone. If he listens to you, you have gained your brother.' "

In this connection Jesus goes even further. When Peter asked, " 'Lord, how often shall my brother sin against me, and I forgive him? As many as seven times?' Jesus said to him, 'I do not say to you seven times, but seventy times seven.' " Scholars agree on the interpretation of this passage. Jesus is saying that we are not to keep books on the number of times we have been wronged by another, but that the process of forgiveness is to go on indefinitely. We are not to count the times we forgive. There is no limit to what the religious man must do to perfect reconciliation or right relationship with his fellow man.

Love Your Enemy

Jesus cast aside the old idea that neighbors are to be loved and enemies are to be hated, insisting that enemies are to be loved because such is the will of God. The triangular relationship includes not only man, his neighbor, and God, but man, his enemy, and God. " 'You have heard that it was said, "You shall love your neighbor and hate your enemy." But I say to you, Love your enemies and pray for those who persecute you.' " The reason given is " 'that you may be sons of your Father who is in heaven; for he makes his sun rise on the evil and on the good, and sends rain on the just and on the unjust' " *Matthew* 5:43-45.

Man Never Stands Alone

It is safe to say that, in the thinking and acting of Jesus, man never stands alone before God. With him are his relationships with and attitudes toward white men, black men, red men, yellow men, and brown men; toward the rich and the poor, the great and the small; toward the learned and the unlearned; toward friends and enemies.

This point is made no clearer anywhere in the whole Bible than it is in the judgment scene as set forth in the twenty-fifth chapter of *Matthew*. We are to be judged by God now and always on the basis of our attitudes toward and our treatment of one another. This teaching is universal in its application; it cuts across the barriers of class, race, and nation.

It seems quite obvious that the test would have been different if the church leaders of Jesus' time had been setting up the conditions under which one was to inherit the kingdom of God. The scribes and the Pharisees in all probability would have laid considerable emphasis upon the keeping of the letter of the law, the dotting of the *i*'s and the crossing of the *t*'s. They would have insisted that no work be done on the Sabbath Day, not even deeds of mercy such as giving sight to the blind and healing of the sick. The aristocratic Sadducees would have wanted to know how careful the candidate had been in observing the rituals of correct procedure. The Zealots would have required that one believe in and adhere to the principles of revolution and violence before being admitted into the kingdom.

One applying in the fourth century for membership in the Christian community would have been tested on the relationship of Father, Son, and Holy Ghost, and in the fifth on the human and the divine natures of Christ. We would not for a moment minimize the significance of the theological controversies of the fourth and fifth centuries. These tests were essential, for without the acceptance of such Christian doctrines the Christian movement would have been destroyed by heretical men.

Church leaders of our own time carry out different entrance requirements for membership in their churches. Roman Catholics have certain requirements for membership, the various Protestant bodies others. Some zealous church people of our day would and do make membership in the white race the basis upon which one can join their local church.

Some groups might contend that wealth, social position, and family background should be taken into account. It is conceivable that if these people were to make the decision on who could qualify for admission into the kingdom of God, in the final judgment, they would insist on the requirements of their respective church bodies. The question of just and harmonious relationship with man might never be raised, although Jesus, the author of Christianity, never lost sight of the primary importance of man's relationship to his brother.

"You Did It to Me"

In his characteristic way, Jesus goes to the very heart of the matter by making it clear that one qualifies to inherit the kingdom when he combines the love of God with the love of man and when he is conscious of the fact that he serves God when he serves man. The two cannot be separated. The formula is a simple one:

" ' "Come, O blessed of my Father, inherit the kingdom prepared for you from the foundation of the world; for I was hungry and you gave me food, I was thirsty and you gave me drink, I was a stranger and you welcomed me, I was naked and you clothed me, I was sick and you visited me, I was in prison and you came to me." Then the righteous will answer him, "Lord, when did we see thee hungry and feed thee, or thirsty and give thee drink? And when did we see thee a stranger and welcome thee, or naked and clothe thee? And when did we see thee sick or in prison and visit thee?" And the King will answer them, "Truly, I say to you, as you did it to one of the least of these my brethren, you did it to me" ' " *Matthew* 25:34-40.

Jesus and Zacchaeus

In the nineteenth chapter of the *Gospel According to Luke,* we have the story of Zacchaeus, "a chief tax collector, and rich."

Tax collectors for the Roman government were disliked by the Jews, many of whom thought it unlawful to pay tribute to a foreign power. Collecting taxes is not always a pleasant task even when in the employ of one's own government. Tax collectors in Jesus' day were not considered to be very honest, and, besides, Zacchaeus was collecting taxes from his own people, perhaps to pay for the Roman army of occupation. Some say that the publicans were not allowed to come into the temple or synagogue, to take part in public prayers, or to testify in a court of justice.

It is probably true that Zacchaeus bargained with the Roman officials to collect a certain amount of taxes and that what he collected above the amount agreed upon he kept for himself. For example, if he had agreed to collect $100,000 and then collected $200,000, his profit was 100 per cent.

Then, in his contact with Jesus, Zacchaeus had a

change of heart with respect to his place and duty in society. When he repented of his sins and set about to heal the wounds he had inflicted, Jesus declared that salvation had come to him.

Zacchaeus stated first his intention to give half of his goods to the poor. He went further and said he would restore fourfold to any man he had wronged by taking too much from him (*Luke* 19:8). In other words, Zacchaeus said, "If I have collected one dollar too much in taxes from the poor widow across the way, I will return to her four dollars. If I have collected one hundred dollars too much from the rich man, I will return to him four hundred dollars."

If I understand Jesus correctly, he says that regardless of the many bad things that a person has done, he can be forgiven when with God's help he repents of his sins, stops doing the wrong things, and sets about to restore the losses and repair the damage done. Zacchaeus did this, and in doing it he was doing the will of God and relating himself aright to God and to man.

Taking the First Step

All of us should seek to restore right relations with anyone who holds anything against us. Jesus makes this very plain. When something goes wrong, it is the man whose heart is right who is to take the first step. The words in *Matthew* 5:22-24 are our guide at this point.

How significant it is that Jesus places the responsibility for getting the thing right upon the man who holds no grudge or hatred against the other fellow. Ordinarily one would expect Jesus to place the responsibility upon the man who is angry. Not so. He places it where it belongs. He places it upon the man whose heart is pure, whose hands are clean. Only a man whose heart is right can reclaim a man whose heart is not right. Thieves do not convert thieves. Gamblers are not sent to put on a revival for gamblers. A man who does not like Negroes or Indians is not likely to be sent as a missionary to work among them.

Fellowship with God as well as fellowship with other persons was tragically broken in three high schools of two Western cities where the prejudice against Negro students ran so high that many white students went on strike demanding segregated schools. It was broken again when the superintendent of a high school in another city refused to honor a contract between the school board and a brilliant young woman when it was discovered that she had a Negro ancestor. It was broken when Autherine Lucy sought to matriculate in the University of Alabama. It was broken when a few children in the District of Columbia, Baltimore, and a town in Delaware went on strike because of integration in the school resulting from the May 17, 1954, decision of the United States Supreme Court, which declared segregation in the public school unconstitutional. It is being broken wherever and whenever state officials lead a program of rebellion against the decision of the Supreme Court. It was broken when a fourteen-year-old boy was murdered in Mississippi. Anyone who reads the New Testament must understand that no man is right with God who is not right with man. And yet how strange it is that this aspect of the life and teachings of Jesus has become such a neglected area in our daily practices.

5.

race prejudice—a wicked thing

Prejudice is a terrible thing. Race prejudice is a curse to anyone who is afflicted with it. The word prejudice means a premature judgment, a bias, usually an unreasoning objection to a person or thing—or to a particular race. It means to form an opinion, usually unfavorable, before the examination of the facts. It clogs understanding and makes us unfair to those for whom it is entertained. Prejudice is based on feeling rather than reasoning and understanding.

The prejudiced mind ignores the facts, however real and convincing. Prejudice against a race or group is usually passed on from one generation to another, from parents to children, and from adults to young people. It is spread and perpetuated through books, newspapers, movies, and speeches. Children are born without race prejudice, but they are apt to develop prejudices held by their parents, older brothers and sisters, and teachers, and others with whom they come in contact.

Prejudice against a particular race leads to segregation and discrimination. To segregate means to set apart, to separate from others, to cut off from the main body. Segregation may be accomplished either by law or custom. Of the two, legal segregation is the most damaging. In the United States racial segregation means the erection of religious, political, economic, and social barriers between one ethnic or racial group and another, making it forever impossible for members of the two groups fully to know, appreciate, and understand each other. It inevitably leads to discrimination, which is a difference in treatment of two or more persons, usually unfair in favor of one side.

Segregation Hurts the Segregated

Usually the question is: What does discrimination or segregation do to the person segregated, to the disadvantaged person? It is clear that segregation and discrimination hurt the pride of the person discriminated against; that they often retard his mental, moral, and physical development; and that they rob society of what the disadvantaged person or group might contribute to enrich the community. Segregation crushes manhood, creates fear in the segregated, and makes him cowardly. It develops in the person segregated a feeling of inferiority to the extent that he never knows what his capabilities are. His mind is never free to develop unrestricted. The ceiling and not the sky becomes the limit of his striving. Segregation and discrimination make men slaves in their minds, and God did not make men to be slaves. He made them to be free and to walk the earth with dignity, not to cringe and kowtow.

Under a segregated system, a few men can and do rise above the system and are free and able, despite crippling circumstances. But the vast majority of segregated men can hardly overcome the handicaps that segregation and discrimination impose upon them. Segregation has made thousands of Negroes feel that they are "nobodies" and that they have no right to aspire to nobler things. A German, after traveling through America and seeing what segregation has done to the soul of the Negro, expressed the opinion that the segregation and discrimination that have been inflicted upon the Negro in this country through the decades have been more damaging to the Negro than the death that Hitler inflicted was to the Jews.

Segregation on the basis of color or race is a wicked thing because it penalizes a person for being what God has made him and for conditions over which he has no control. If one were segregated because of ignorance, he could learn and change the situation. If one were segregated because of poverty, he could work and improve his economic status. If he were segregated because of uncleanliness, he could bathe and become acceptable. But if one is segregated and stigmatized because of his race, he is penalized for something that he cannot change. And to do this is tantamount to saying to God, "You made a mistake, God, when you made people of different races and colors." Segregation based on color and race is a great sin. It is not only a sin against man, it is a sin against God.

Discrimination Degrades the Segregator

Lest this end up as a one-sided picture, let us see what segregation and discrimination do to the person who imposes them upon another. We seldom think of this phase of the subject. We seem to feel that damage is done only to the person discriminated against or the person segregated. Discrimination scars the soul of the segregator as well as the soul of the segregated. When we build fences to keep others out, erect barriers to keep others down, deny to others the freedom that we ourselves enjoy and cherish most, we keep ourselves in, hold ourselves down, and erect barriers against others that become prison bars to our own souls. Booker T. Washington was so right when he said, in essence, that you cannot keep a man down in a ditch unless you stay in the ditch with him to keep him there.

None of us grow to the mental and moral stature of free men if we view life with prejudiced eyes for, thereby, we shut our minds to truth and reality, which are essential to spiritual, mental, and moral growth. The time we should spend in creative activity, we waste on small things that dwarf the mind and stultify the soul. Prejudice is both economically and psychologically wasteful.

If a university is staffed with men who are steeped in prejudice against racial or religious groups, against national or ethnic groups, it will never become a truly great university. Whether working in the physical sciences, the social sciences, philosophy, religion, or literature, the mind must be free to pursue truth objectively and unafraid. For the mind to develop to the maximum, it must develop in a free atmosphere, unhampered by racial or ethnic prejudice. The scholar is in pursuit of truth, and his mind should not be circumscribed.

Race prejudice is a wicked thing because the prejudiced adult mind passes its prejudice on to the innocent young mind, which is born without prejudice of any kind. Thus, at an early age a potentially brilliant mind may be so restricted that it will never grow to full maturity.

Race prejudice in the minds of the dominant group makes the people of that group cruel, unfair, and afraid. It creates in them a feeling of superiority and a feeling that the members of the "inferior" group can be pushed around at the will of the dominant group. Segregation and prejudice are responsible for much of the physical brutality that minority groups suffer at the hands of the group in control. They are responsible for the laws of segregation and other discriminatory laws designed to keep certain racial groups in "their place." The group in control is partly responsible for the inferior economic status of Negroes. There are jobs and positions Negroes cannot hold, even when competent, and there are positions they cannot train for. Segregation and prejudice account for many inequalities in education that have been practiced in this country for decades. The nine justices of the Supreme Court sensed this situation when they said in their May 17, 1954, decision: "We conclude that in the field of public education the doctrine of 'separate but equal' has no place. Separate educational facilities are inherently unequal."

This is so because the first objective of segregation is to place a legal badge of inferiority upon the segregated and to brand him as unfit to move freely among other human beings. This badge says the segregated is mentally, morally, and socially unfit to move around as a free man. And if segregation continues long enough, thousands among the segregated will come to believe that they are inferior. The second objective of segregation is to set the segregated apart so that he can be treated as an inferior—set apart in the courts, in recreation, in transportation, in politics, in government, in employment, in housing, in religion, in education, in hotels, in motels, in restaurants, and in every other area of American life. With one group having all the power and possessing and controlling all the tax money, human nature being what it is, inequality is inherent in segregation.

The racially prejudiced mind cannot deal fairly with the group against whom its prejudice is directed. In a rigidly segregated community, it is hardly possible for a member of the segregated group to receive justice in the courts if the case involves a member of the dominant race. Even prominent men are afraid to do what they know is right. Lawyers can hardly present their cases without bias. Judges and jurors can hardly judge with complete objectivity. Ministers are afraid to speak out.

Who then is hurt? Both are seriously hurt, the person who segregates and inflicts discrimination and the person who is the victim, the man who is held down and the man who holds him down. Both are slaves to a system that binds both the oppressor and the oppressed.

Discrimination Discredits Us Abroad

Segregation based on race and color is an unfortunate thing because it weakens our influence and prestige abroad. I have referred to the observation of a German visitor who compared America's treatment of Negroes with Hitler's treatment of the Jews. Although we try to be Christian toward colored people who visit us from Asia, we are too frequently not equally Christian toward colored people who come to us from Africa. Recently, a group of foreign students, mostly from countries where people have darker skins—India, Pakistan, the Philippines, Haiti, Africa, Lebanon—visited a Southern city.

Their project required that the group eat together and stay together. The colored students from Asia were housed in hotels downtown. Students from Africa and Haiti were segregated on the campus of a Negro college. The young women from Africa and Haiti protested and left the project. Doubtless they related this unfortunate incident when they returned to their respective countries. It does not help our international relations.

On the whole, visitors from all other lands except Africa and the West Indies are treated better in the United States than Negro Americans. And yet the eyes and minds of the colored visitors who come to our shores are not closed. As long as Negroes are segregated and discriminated against in the United States, we are going to have a difficult time convincing the world that we are sincere when we preach Christianity and talk democracy.

When I went to India in 1936 and 1937 to attend a world conference of the Young Men's Christian Association, I found that the Indian people were vitally interested in the racial situation in this country. Everywhere I spoke they wanted to know about segregation and the Negro. At a school for India's untouchables, I was introduced as an "untouchable" from the United States. The professor who introduced me was using me as an example of what an untouchable might become. At first he angered me by calling me an "untouchable," but I soon realized that he was right. As long as Negroes are prohibited from voting in some areas of the South, denied employment in certain fields, segregated in housing, not permitted to worship in some churches, and denied equal educational opportunities, they are America's "untouchables."

When I returned to India in 1952 and 1953 to attend meetings of the Central Committee of the World Council of Churches, I believe the Indians were more keenly interested in the question of race than they were in 1936 and 1937. Mrs. Mays and I were shocked to see a sign at the exclusive Taj Mahal Hotel in Bombay: "No South Africans permitted." It was the Indian way of resenting what the South African Government was doing to Indians, Bantus, and colored or mixed people. Every high Indian official who spoke to the Central Committee, including Prime Minister Nehru and Radhakrishnan, the philosopher and vice-president of India, made strong comments on the race problem, with special reference to South Africa and the United States.

In Lucknow I held a press conference with nine newspapermen from different parts of India. They wanted to discuss nothing except the racial situation in the United States and South Africa. They cross-examined me for ninety minutes. When I told them that the racial situation in the United States had greatly improved since I was in India in 1937, they demanded proof. Fortunately, I could tell them truthfully that lynching is almost a thing of the past, that educational opportunities are being equalized, that new jobs are opening up to Negroes, that Negroes are now enrolled in nearly every state university of the South, and that Negro and white Americans are worshiping together in increasing numbers in our churches. It was not easy to convince them that I was telling the truth.

I addressed a Y.M.C.A. group in Columbo, Ceylon. An old gentleman who questioned me about Negroes and communism thought I was lying when I told him that there were very few Communists among Negroes in the United States. He commented that the way Negroes are treated in this country all of them should be Communists. When I told him that Negroes did not need to become Communists because we are making great progress in race relations, he was still unconvinced.

It is no exaggeration when I say that there are a billion people in Asia who are sensitive to the race problem in the United States and to the way Negroes, Indians, Chinese, and Japanese, as well as Puerto Ricans, Mexicans, and Jews, are treated in this country. And make no mistake, the Communists will continue to play up our shortcomings in this area, and they will continue to minimize our virtues.

6.

the church and race

The church in America is a unique institution. No other institution in the United States makes the claim for itself that the church makes. Practically every church of whatever denomination would deny the assumption that it is merely an earthly institution, created solely by man. The Christian church everywhere accepts as valid *Matthew* 16:15-18 as evidence of its divine origin. When Jesus asked his disciples, " 'But who do you say that I am?' Simon Peter replied, 'You are the Christ, the Son of the living God.' And Jesus answered him, 'Blessed are you, Simon Bar-Jona! For flesh and blood has not revealed this to you, but my Father who is in heaven.' " Then Jesus said, " 'And I tell you, you are Peter, and on this rock I will build my church. . . .' "

The Christian church would also deny the allegation that its ultimate and final allegiance is to man. The church in America does not accept even the state as being an object worthy of supreme devotion. If one's ultimate allegiance is to God and if the church is ordained of God, in the very nature of its existence the church cannot wholly conform to the ways of the world. There must be tension between it and the world.

As a worshiping institution no church can justify on the basis of race the exclusion from its worship of anyone who has a sincere desire to worship God. Language or liturgy or ritual may make one voluntarily separate himself from a particular church or creed, but this action should be a choice on the part of the worshiper and not a restriction imposed upon him by the group. A church has a right to set up its own creed or profession of faith, but whoever accepts that formulation of faith should never be denied admission. There should be no denial of worship or membership to any Baptist, Methodist, Congregational Christian, Presbyterian, Episcopalian, Roman Catholic, or anyone else who subscribes to the faith of the church he wishes to join. Churches exist on the basis of common profession of faith.

In the area of worship and membership, the criteria of admission to the Christian church should never be based on race. This is not a matter of coercion or pressure. It is simply a matter of every church making it clear to the world that the church is God's house, not man's, and that whoever wishes to worship there, in sincerity and truth, is free to do so. But this assertion is not enough. The basis of membership should be applicable to all peoples. One should be accepted on his profession of faith.

In December, 1936, I was traveling from Palestine to Egypt in a compartment with an Arab who was a devout Muslim. As is usually the case when one converses with colored people in other parts of the world, my Arab companion wanted to know about Negro-white relations in the United States. He asked if there were segregated churches in the United States based on race and color, churches that would deny membership to a Negro. I told him there were many churches, not all, in the United States where this was true. He then wanted to know if Negroes and whites belonged to the same religious faith. I told him that both Negroes and whites are Christians. He asked me more than once if any Negroes were Christians. After affirming again and again that Negroes and whites embrace the same Christian faith, he said, "I do not comprehend. When one accepts the Muslim faith, race and nationality do not count against him."

The Old Testament Does Not Support Segregation

Space does not permit extensive documentation of this point. Considerable evidence has already been given in the preceding pages. It must be said, however, that the best biblical scholars in this country and Europe say that the church cannot find shelter in the Bible for defense of racial segregation in its congregation. In the Old Testament where lines are definitely and sharply drawn, they are drawn along religious lines and not along the lines of race and color. For example, the nations that surrounded Israel belonged to the same racial stock as Israel. The Moabites shared Israel's language, the Edomites were tied to Israel by bonds of blood, and the Canaanites lived in the same country. But as long as these peoples served their own gods, they were not accepted by Israel. On the other hand, the Gideonites, who accepted Israel's God, ultimately became Israelites.

What About Genesis 9?

Were it not for the fact that the mythical interpretation of *Genesis* 9:18-27 is still being erroneously used by the uninformed to justify segregating the Negro, we would omit reference to the Ham story. But since there may be some who are not familiar with this *Genesis* story, we discuss it briefly here. The argument goes that Noah placed a curse upon Ham and the latter became black. We invite the reader to read the whole of the ninth and tenth chapters of *Genesis*. It does not take an expert in the Old Testament to discover that this interpretation of the Noah-Ham story is completely false.

In the first place, Noah placed the curse and not God, and Noah was coming out of a drunken stupor when he announced the curse. We doubt if God would use a drunken man to place a curse upon a people. We do not accept as authority a statement by a drunken man. The curse was laid upon Ham's son, Canaan, and not upon Ham and it was not the curse of color. Verse 21 of the ninth chapter says plainly that Noah "drank of the wine, and became drunk, and lay uncovered in his tent." Verses 24 and 25 read:

"When Noah awoke from his wine and knew what his youngest son had done to him, he said, 'Cursed be Canaan; a slave of slaves shall he be to his brothers.'" Nothing is said here about his becoming "black."

The Bible and science agree that life began in unity. We did not have three different origins for the three major human groups: Caucasoids, Negroids, and Mongoloids.

Furthermore, there is nothing in the Bible story to connect the descendants of the cursed Canaan with Africa. Verse 19 of the tenth chapter of *Genesis* says:

"And the territory of the Canaanites extended from Sidon, in the direction of Gerar, as far as Gaza, and in the direction of Sodom, Gomorrah, Admah, and Zeboi-

im, as far as Lasha." In the history of biblical interpretation, I know of no first-rate scholar who connects the
Negro with Ham, whose son Canaan was cursed by
Noah as the eponymous ancestor of the Canaanites. The
Land of Canaan was once the name of modern Palestine,
today partitioned by the United Nations into Israel and
the Hashemite Kingdom of Jordan. The Ham story has
no connection with the Negro and none with Africa.
When considering this passage, the reader should not
forget that through a long history the Israelites hated the
Canaanites. One author points out that the story of the
curse on Canaan may purport to explain the success of
Israel in subduing the Canaanites, "whose eponymous
ancestor had been cursed for an act of filial impiety."

The New Testament Does Not Support Segregation

In the New Testament it is equally clear that separate-
ness was on the basis of religion and culture and not on
the ground of race or ethnic origin. From the beginning
of his career, Jesus proclaimed a religion that was supra-
racial, supranational, supracultural, and supraclass. His
doctrine of God as father embraces the human race and
makes us all children of the same God. God is our father,
and we are his children.

When we pray, "Our Father who art in heaven," we
acknowledge our kinship in him. His concern for all of
his children is so great that the very hairs on their heads
are numbered. He watches over the sparrow, the most
insignificant of birds, which is cited as proof that his concern for his children is much greater. In his message to
the twelve when he sent them forth, Jesus said:

" '. . . do not fear those who kill the body but cannot

kill the soul; rather fear him who can destroy both soul and body in hell. Are not two sparrows sold for a penny? And not one of them will fall to the ground without your Father's will. But even the hairs of your head are all numbered. Fear not, therefore; you are of more value than many sparrows' " *Matthew* 10:28-31.

The Apostle Paul made the growth and spread of the Christian church possible by making it plain that one did not have to be adopted into the Jewish community in order to belong to the Christian church.

The Early Church Did Not Practice Discrimination

It is clear that a new community was created at Pentecost. The church was born. Jews and proselytes gathered together, and representatives of fifteen different nations were assembled.

This point is made plain in *Acts* 2:1, 9-11:

"When the day of Pentecost had come, they were all together in one place . . . . Parthians and Medes and Elamites and residents of Mesopotamia, Judea and Cappadocia, Pontus and Asia, Phrygia and Pamphylia, Egypt and the parts of Libya belonging to Cyrene, and visitors from Rome, both Jews and proselytes, Cretans and Arabians."

Church historians and New Testament scholars agree that from its inception the Christian church had in its membership people of different nations, races, and colors. Nowhere in the early church do we find distinctions drawn on the basis of country or race. *James* 2:1-6 condemns the separation of cultural and social groups in the local church. What was true of the early church was true of the church of the Middle Ages. In both the ancient and

47

medieval church, the basis of membership was faith not race, Christ not color, creedal acceptance not nationality.

Science Does Not Support the Church in Segregation

A UNESCO publication *The Race Concept,* points out:

"In matters of race, the only characteristics which anthropologists have so far been able to use effectively as a basis for classification are physical, anatomical and physiological. Available scientific knowledge provides no basis for believing that the groups of mankind differ in their innate capacity for intellectual and emotional development. Some biological differences between human beings within a single race may be as great as or greater than the same biological differences between races."[1]

In another connection the United Nations publication, *What is Race?,* speaks for modern science on race:

". . . all of us believed that the biological differences found amongst human racial groups can in no case justify the views of racial inequality which have been based on ignorance and prejudice, and that all of the differences which we know can well be disregarded for all ethical human purposes."[2]

How Did We Get This Way?

Race and color did not count in the early existence of the Protestant church. It was when modern Western

[1]*The Race Concept.* Paris, United Nations Educational, Scientific, and Cultural Organization, 1952, p. 15. Used by permission.
[2]*What Is Race?,* by Diana Tead. Paris, UNESCO, 1952, p. 82. Used by permission.

imperialism began to explore and exploit the colored peoples of Africa, Asia, and America that segregation and discrimination based on color and race was initiated. It was then that color was first associated with "inferiority," and white with "superiority." The report of the section on The Church Amid Racial and Ethnic Tensions at the sessions of the World Council of Churches at Evanston in 1954, said:

"The broad pattern of major racial group tensions which trouble the world today had its historical origins in the period of European overseas exploration and expansion into America, Asia, and Africa. The resulting exploitation of one group by another, involving groups differing in race, varied on the three continents. But the same general relations of asserted superiority and inferiority developed between the white world and the colored world. Color became first the symbol and then the accepted characteristic of the intergroup tensions."

World Council of Churches Expresses Concern

If segregation in the churches based on race and color is a modern thing, what are the practices of the churches today? When the churches of the world meet in conference, there is no segregation of racial and ethnic groups. Not only is there no segregation nor discrimination based on race or color in world gatherings, but in every world conference since 1928 the practice of segregation in the church has been strongly condemned. These conferences have gone on record against it: the International Missionary Council at Jerusalem in 1928 and Madras in 1938, the World Conference on Faith and Order at Edinburgh in 1937 and the World Conference on Life and Work at

Oxford the same year, the First Assembly of the World Council of Churches at Amsterdam in 1948, the Third World Conference on Faith and Order at Lund in 1952, the World Council of Churches through its Central Committee at Toronto in 1950 and at Lucknow in 1952-53, and the Second Assembly of the World Council of Churches at Evanston in 1954. In world gatherings the churches have completely removed the color bar from their worship and membership. Section III of the First Assembly of the World Council of Churches at Amsterdam in 1948 went on record as follows:

"It [the church] knows that it must call society away from prejudice based upon race or color, and from the practices of discrimination and segregation as denials of justice and human dignity, but it cannot say a convincing word to society unless it takes steps to eliminate these practices from the Christian community because they contradict all that it believes about God's love for all his children."

The World Council at Evanston in 1954 said:

"The Second Assembly of the World Council of Churches declares its conviction that the principle of racial segregation is incompatible with the idea of a Christian society. With even greater concern the Assembly declares its conviction that the principle of racial segregation is incompatible with the nature of the Church of Christ in whom differences of race are already transcended. It, therefore, calls upon the churches within its membership to proclaim and work for the abolition of barriers of racial segregation within society at large. At the same time the Council confirms its renunciation of the principle of racial discrimination within its own organization and commends to the member churches that they seek by study and administrative action to remove any forms of racial discrimination which may exist within their own organization."

National Church Bodies Denounce Segregation

The color bar has been almost removed on the national church scene in the United States. The Federal Council, now a part of the National Council of the Churches of Christ in the United States of America, speaking on this subject in 1946 had this to say:

"The Federal Council of Churches of Christ in America hereby renounces the pattern of segregation in race relations as unnecessary and undesirable and a violation of the gospel of love and human brotherhood. Having taken this action, the Federal Council requests its constituent communions to do likewise. As proof of their sincerity in this renunciation they will work for a non-segregated church and a nonsegregated society."

The National Council of the Churches of Christ in the United States of America, representing thirty national religious bodies, has more recently spoken out in equally strong terms. As a rule national denominational bodies have taken the same position.

When three Methodist bodies merged in 1939 to form The Methodist Church, they followed the pattern of segregation and set up a Central Jurisdiction for Negroes. The Methodist Church made progress toward the elimination of segregation in the summer of 1956, however, when the General Conference recommended "that discrimination or segregation by any method or practice whether by conference structure or otherwise in The

Methodist Church be abolished with reasonable speed."
The United Presbyterian Church of North America also
voted for complete integration of all churches, agencies,
and institutions.

It is unfortunate, however, that churches with members in both the North and the South still are not able to
assemble as national bodies in some cities without meet-
ing the monster, segregation.

Local Practices Differ

There are local churches in the North and South where
the color bar does not exist. For example, for many years
Riverside Church in New York City has been open to all
races. Nonsegregation is practiced in both Negro and
white churches in many other places. The Community
Church in Chapel Hill, North Carolina, is open to all
races. The fact that this church is in the heart of the
South gives this special significance.

The March 19, 1956, issue of the *New York Times*
carried a story and pictures of Negroes and whites of two
Presbyterian churches worshiping together in New York.
"More than one hundred members of the Madison Avenue Presbyterian Church at Seventy-third Street wor-
shiped in the modern brick Church of the Master, 360
West 122 Street. About a hundred members of the latter
church attended the 11 A.M. service in the imposing
Madison Avenue edifice."

Despite these noteworthy examples and many others
that could be given, it is in local churches, both North
and South, that the barriers of race are largely in opera-
tion. A decade ago a consultant in race relations esti-
mated that "only one-half of 1 per cent of the Negro-

Protestant Christians in the United States worship regularly in churches with fellow Christians of another race." In *The Protestant Church and the Negro,* Frank Loescher says: "Negro membership appears to be confined to less than 1 per cent of the white churches."[1] The picture now is brighter. Nevertheless, the percentage of local churches in the United States that would deny membership to Negroes is disturbingly high.

If the church practices segregation, it is more blameworthy than a business that operates a segregated streetcar, bus, train, motel, hotel, restaurant, or department store; more blameworthy than men who operate segregated recreational centers such as dance halls, golf clubs, swimming pools, theaters, and motion picture houses. It is difficult to refute the argument that the church is one of the most highly segregated institutions in the United States. It is often more rigidly segregated than professional baseball, professional boxing, certain labor unions, organized gambling, and the organized illegal liquor traffic. Since the May 1, 1954, decision of the Supreme Court, it is conceivable that secular schools and other institutions will desegregate faster than the local churches.

State Laws Pose Problems

The thing that makes the improvement of racial relations so difficult is the fact that segregation has been established by law and in state constitutions. Most churchmen feel that the law must be obeyed, even when they know that a law is an unjust one. Once a law has

[1] *The Protestant Church and the Negro,* by Frank Loescher. New York, Association Press, 1948, p. 77. Used by permission.

And yet since May 31, 1955, White Citizens Councils and other organizations have sprung up with their avowed purpose the maintenance of segregation in the public schools. Some states have passed nullification acts declaring the Supreme Court decision null and void. Five Southern states have now called for interposition. One hundred Southern Congressmen have signed a manifesto declaring that they will do everything they can do legally to get the Supreme Court decision outlawing segregation in the public schools set aside. Negroes have lost their jobs, and some have been threatened because they petitioned their school boards to desegregate the schools. Economic boycotts have been applied to Negroes who petitioned school boards to desegregate the schools. Laws have been passed to the effect that teachers will lose their jobs if they are members of the National Association for the Advancement of Colored People. Texas and Arkansas are making a small beginning to comply with the Court's order. Oklahoma is moving forward.

These threats against Negroes and these attempts to discredit the Supreme Court are serious matters. They strike at one of the basic principles of American democracy. Our government protects the rights of minorities both in the Constitution and through the Supreme Court. If the Court is not to be obeyed and if citizens are denied the right of petition, minorities have no means of seeking redress for injustice suffered.

What are churchmen to do about this rebellious attitude of several Southern states? Most of the national and regional church bodies have called upon the people to obey the edict of the Supreme Court. And yet the local churches of these denominations, with some minor exceptions, do not permit Negroes to join their churches and are silent on the Court's decision. How can the church in good faith urge compliance with the Supreme Court decision and at the same time segregate in its worship? What is the responsibility of the church leaders and all Christians? Are they to speak out or keep quiet, act or do nothing?

I do not propose to tell the churches what they should do. But I do believe a little history will help us to understand the problem. We brought this situation upon ourselves. We here in the South have said all along that we believe in segregation but equal segregation. In 1896 in the Louisiana transportation case, Plessy versus Ferguson, the United States Supreme Court confirmed the "separate but equal" doctrine. But from 1896 to 1935 practically nothing was done to make the "separate" "equal." It is unfortunate to have to record that though the various state constitutions call for racial equality under the law and the Supreme Court confirmed the doctrine of "separate but equal" in 1896, no serious efforts were put forth to equalize educational opportunities for Negroes until suits began to be filed in the courts beginning in 1935. In other words, the Southern states did not obey the decision of the Supreme Court in 1896. They did not obey it in transportation nor in any other area. From 1896 to 1935, a period of thirty-nine years, little, if anything, was done to equalize educational opportunities for Negroes in the South.

For example, according to a 1931 issue of *The Christian Century*, thirteen Southern states during the school year, 1918-19, spent $12.91 per capita for each white child of school age, $4.42 for each Negro child—a difference of $8.49. During the school year, 1924-25, these thirteen states spent $27.95 per capita for each white child of school age, for the Negro child $9.52—a difference of $18.43. In 1931, these thirteen states were spending per capita for each white child of school age $40.92, for the Negro child $15.78—a difference of $25.14. In other words, from 1919 up to 1931, the per capita expenditure for the white child increased $28.01, for the Negro child, $11.36.

It is not surprising, therefore, that the various surveys prove that the education Negroes receive in the segregated public schools of the South is, in most instances, inferior to that received by the whites. It will take many decades for the Negro to overcome the handicaps in his education. Commenting on the point of inequality in segregation, Eli Ginzberg in *The Negro Potential* writes:

"Because of deficiencies in their home and community environments and in the schools they attend, Negroes have far less opportunity to acquire a solid education than do most of the white population among whom they live. A man's education is exceedingly important in determining his eventual position on the economic scale."[1]

When, in 1935, Donald G. Murray won his case in the Appellate Court of Maryland to enter the University of Maryland Law School, the South knew that it had to move toward equalization. Since 1935 many suits have been won in Federal courts ruling that school facilities must be made equal. The recent moves toward equalizing educational opportunities for Negroes were stimulated

[1]*The Negro Potential,* by Eli Ginzberg. New York, Columbia University Press, 1956, p. 42. Used by permission.

mainly by victories won in the Federal courts. Great strides have been made, but the gulf of inequality still exists.

It would have been a mighty fine thing if we had obeyed the Supreme Court in 1896, not only in transportation but in education as well. If we had done that, the problem would have been solved because gradually the separate school system would have been abolished and we would have been saved from the agony and fear of this hour. But if, as the Supreme Court says and as experience proves, inequality is inherent in segregation, the doctrine of "separate but equal" is a contradiction. To expect equality in segregation is to expect too much of unregenerated human nature. How strange! We did not try to obey the Supreme Court in 1896; we do not want to obey it now. What is the Christian's responsibility?

7.

beyond knowledge

Many people are disturbed about God because their faith in him has been shaken. They raise questions that were raised centuries ago: Why do the wicked prosper and the righteous suffer? Why doesn't God rise up in his power and do something about the world? How can a God of love, justice, and mercy permit war, injustice, and exploitation?

Other people are disturbed about the Devil. They attribute a good bit of what is happening in the world to the Devil.

Man, the Disturbing Factor

The disturbing factor, however, is not the Devil, which we spell with a capital *D*, and certainly not God, but man. It is people who keep the world in confusion and chaos.

How can we make man good, unselfish, loving, and kind? What can we do with strong nations so that they will not want to take advantage of weak nations? What can we do with races so that no race will want privileges for itself that it would not gladly share with another? How can war be abolished?

Two Ways to Make Man Good

There are two ways through which human nature can be improved. One is through the process of education, both formal and informal, the other is through religion. We seem to have used both of these processes poorly to make man the kind of person he ought to be. History shows that man builds great civilizations, but, in turn, he destroys the civilizations that he builds. We did a good job in World War II destroying a lot of what we call modern civilization.

Man Is a Paradox

There is a contradiction in man that is disturbing. He has inherent in his nature elements of the divine. He also has inherent in his nature elements of the Devil. Man may be good or evil, honest or dishonest, sinner or saint, kind or unkind, loving or unloving, just or unjust. Man is capable of building a heaven or a hell on earth.

There is not any sure way of determining which of these natures is going to predominate. This is true because in making man a free person rather than a machine, God gave man the power of choice, the power to decide for himself between good and evil.

Knowledge Does Not Insure Goodness

It is disturbing to realize that when we increase in knowledge, we do not necessarily increase in goodness or sense of values. We used to believe that people did the destructive or brutal thing because they did not know any better. We believed that nations fought wars because their knowledge was limited. We believed that it was all a matter of education and that once man saw the light, he would follow it; that once he knew the truth, he would tell it; and that once he could distinguish the high road from the low road, he would take the high one.

We know now that it is not as simple as that. Men can know the truth and lie. Men can know the ways of peace and deliberately plan war. Socrates believed that men did evil things through ignorance. But the Apostle Paul was wiser than Socrates and nearer the truth when he exclaimed:

"For I do not do the good I want, but the evil I do not want is what I do. Now if I do what I do not want, it is no longer I that do it, but sin which dwells within me. So I find it to be a law that when I want to do right, evil lies close at hand" *Romans* 7:19-21.

Paul was simply saying that he needed something more than intellect, more than knowledge. "Wretched man that I am! Who will deliver me from this body of death? Thanks be to God through Jesus Christ Our Lord! So then, I of myself serve the law of God with my mind, but with my flesh I serve the law of sin" *Romans* 7:24-25.

Freedom comes from religion, from God, through Jesus Christ.

No one can discredit the mind or knowledge, for we must live by the knowledge that man discovers with his mind. But to rely upon the intellect alone is one of the chief sins of our time. There can be no doubting the fact that man has made great strides in developing the human mind. Yet it seems clear that to develop man's mind without in some way developing his goodness and his sense of values is worse than placing a loaded shotgun in the hands of a fool. Knowledge of mathematics does not make a man honest; it does not keep him from robbing a bank. Knowledge of chemistry does not prevent a man from using what he knows for destructive ends. Knowledge of physics does not stop a man from using planes to drop bombs on the innocent.

Look at Germany! History records no nation more brilliant than the German nation. At the turn of the century, Americans had an inferiority complex where the Germans were involved. Many Americans felt that in order to be acclaimed scholars they had to study if only for six weeks at such German universities as those of Berlin, Munich, and Leipzig. Many of the outstanding scholars of the world, especially in science, philosophy, and religion, have been Germans. No one can doubt the intellectual caliber of the German mind. On the other hand, no one can deny that the German leaders prior to and during World War II deliberately trained their youth to be brutal, that they precipitated war, that they were cruel and inhuman in their campaign to conquer the world. In a few years millions of Jews were killed in Germany.

What is said of Germany can be said largely of Japan and in lesser degree of other nations. And we must never forget that the United States was the first to perfect and use the atomic bomb.

The Human Mind Is Treacherous

We have to rely on the mind, but we must remember that the mind is deceptive. We deceive ourselves into thinking that we are rational and objective in our approaches to life, but by and large our emotions, feelings, and desires control our minds. We often do what we want to do, what our feelings and desires suggest. Then we use our minds to justify what we have done. The human mind is capable of justifying to its own satisfaction whatever it wishes to. People of all nations will use their minds to prove that they are no more guilty for World War II than other nations. And they will succeed in convincing themselves and their children that they are right. The United States has sought for decades to justify laws and practices of segregation based solely on race and color. The human mind is treacherous. It tends to prove what it wants to believe.

Knowledge Can Lead to An Impasse

There is a point beyond which knowledge cannot take us. We have already referred to how little knowledge helps when we face the reality of death. One may live a long time, but there comes a time when knowledge fails. The most learned of men is helpless in the sickroom when his wife, son, daughter, or friend is dying.

Men have more learning now than they have ever had before—more mathematics, physics, chemistry, philosophy, social science, and religion than any other generation. Yet we are as confused now as men have ever been at any period in history. We saw a great war coming upon us, but we could not avert it. Germany and Japan were defeated in World War II, but with all our knowledge and learning, we hardly know enough to avoid sowing the seeds of another war. Our economists are well trained, but they cannot determine what kind of economic system we shall have twenty-five years from now. We find ourselves caught in the midst of catastrophe and chaos, and in one sense the Ph.D. is as inadequate as the illiterate and the world statesman stands almost as helpless in shaping world policies as the country politician.

As we have already pointed out, the basic defect is not in knowledge but in man. But even after we become better men and women, the future is not wholly in our hands. The additional is beyond knowledge. Alfred Tennyson sensed the situation perfectly when he wrote in the prologue to his "In Memoriam":

> Let knowledge grow from more to more,
>   But more of reverence in us dwell;
>   That mind and soul, according well,
> May make one music as before,
> But vaster.

John Drinkwater is equally profound when he writes in "A Prayer":

> Knowledge we ask not, knowledge thou hast lent;
> But Lord, the will, there lies our bitter need;
> Give us to build above the deep intent
> The deed, the deed.[1]

The Verdict of Religion

From its origin up to now, the Christian faith has taken the position that man needs God and that without God he cannot be saved. Human nature somehow must be touched by divine nature. The Christian religion has had nineteen centuries in which to transform man. Still the job is unfinished, for man has been free to reject God and has done so. Yet to take from man this right to decide

[1]Copyright © 1919 by John Drinkwater. Reprinted by permission of Samuel French Ltd.

for himself whether to reject or to accept God would be to rob him of elements that build character and mold personality. The hope is that he will decide to accept God.

Rays of Hope

Examples in history and in contemporary life prove that people are really changed for the better under the the impact of religion. The story of the Apostle Paul, told in the ninth chapter of *Acts,* is one of the outstanding examples on record. Paul, a persecutor of the early Christians, became a different individual from that moment on the road to Damascus when the Lord spoke to him. It was the kind of conversion that changed the total man.

Saint Augustine, great Christian bishop and philosopher of the fourth century, was unruly, confused, and skeptical as a boy and young man. Although he was influenced by the Christian teachings of his mother, he did not become a Christian himself until his experience in a garden in Milan. There he heard the voice of a child singing and applied the words to himself as a divine command. After that he and his life were entirely different.

We all know people in our own experiences whom the Christian religion has changed. Now and then we find in our own communities people in education or business, in religion or politics, in the professions or industry, in any of the many essential services in our everyday life, to whom religion has really made a profound difference. As we look farther and study the lives and works of men like Albert Schweitzer of Africa, T. Z. Koo of China, and Toyohiko Kagawa of Japan, we see more clearly the tremendous power of the Christian religion in human lives.

There are enough examples to convince one that

people can be changed. We must believe that. If human nature cannot be changed, men will fight wars forever. Your sons and daughters will fight the next war, and their sons and daughters will fight the war after the next. If we cannot change people, the deadly weapon of race prejudice will keep one race arrayed against another forever. If we cannot change the hearts and minds of men and women, the strong will always take advantage of the weak. If human nature cannot be improved, then of all creatures, man is the most miserable.

The further conquests of science cannot be impeded. In time and space, the world is a small neighborhood. The economic and political dependence of one group upon the other is a fact. Thermonuclear weapons make it all the more imperative that religion change people for the better. Economic, political, and military power can no longer save a nation. The most modern weapons are already common property. Nothing can save us now except repentance, good will, justice, love, and forgiveness.

Christianity has always held that man can be changed. This is the major function of the Christian church. The sad thing about the present day church is that it does not place enough emphasis upon the need for people to change their unchristian behavior when they join the church. The exploiter does not have to stop exploiting. The man who cheats in his business does not have to stop cheating. The man who holds prejudice against white men, Jews, Negroes, and Asians can hold it and be in good standing in the church. Too many churches are trying to be all things to all men. But when the church really gets on its job, the process of changing people takes on added momentum.

The Christian faith not only maintains that conversion is possible through the power of religion, but it insists further that man is not, as some people think, a creature of his environment wholly shackled and chained by custom, law, habit, tradition, and by what other people say and do. It declares that man can break the bonds of his environment, rise above it, and transform it. He cannot do this alone. Knowledge by itself may not enable him to do it. But once he allows God to come into his life, he is no longer a slave to the practices around him. As pessimistic as any Christian may be about man, he can never deny the power of the Christian religion to make men better.

Young people and adults in many churches are aroused today as never before. They are concerned about interracial and social justice and about the prevention of future wars. Many church groups are working on all phases of the questions discussed in this book. Protestant churches are cooperating through the National Council of the Churches of Christ in the United States of America and working together in state and local communities. Christians of all races from many countries are working together through the World Council of Churches and other channels.

There Is Hope in Man

Since man is unique and since God smiled upon him in a special way, there is a spark of divinity in every individual. Herein lies hope. However low a person may sink in the scale, he may always seek again to climb the heights. He may forever reach out for that which is high and noble.

Men cheat and steal on the one hand. On the other, they declare, "honesty is the best policy." Men get drunk and spend their lives in riotous living. At the same time, they insist that temperance is better than intemperance. The strong exploit the weak, but they would hardly want the job of writing a thesis in defense of their exploitation. Men go to war, spend billions, and kill millions. Yet before they can fight the war, they must convince themselves either that it is right to fight it or that it is the lesser of two evils.

Young people may waste their time at school and do many mean or foolish things. Yet at heart each youth wants to do something worthwhile in the world. There is something in each of us that drives us forever toward that which is better, that which will not let us rest content in darkness and sin. Since this is true, man and youth stand always on the verge of conversion as candidates for the kingdom of God. This longing is a part of man's nature. As long as it is so, we do not despair of the possibility that some day man will cease to reject God.

God and Man Exist for Each Other

In Marc Connelly's *Green Pastures*, God creates man and gives him a beautiful paradise in which to live. In the exercise of his freedom, man chooses to walk in darkness. God repents that he made man and decides to destroy him and start all over again. This he does. He repeoples the earth, satisfied now that man will do right. When man still sins, God threatens to destroy him again but finally decides instead to give him a new land, Canaan, in the hope that man will serve him and do right. Man goes wrong.

Repenting that he ever made man, God swears off and comes to the conclusion that he is through with man. A delegation waits on the Lord, begging him to go back to his people. All the while man, contrary and cruel, is calling upon God for help. How typical! Man won't do exactly right, but somehow he wants God's blessing and sanction.

Every time the prophet, Hosea, passes by the window of heaven, God can hear the voice of Hezdrel down on earth—not exactly praying but in some way beseeching God and expressing a great faith that God is with him and his people. Hosea continues to pass by, and the voice of Hezdrel continues to be heard. Finally, God can't stand it any longer. He goes down to earth and talking with Hezdrel discovers that as wicked as the people are, they still have faith in the Lord God of Hosea.

The story means that man cannot leave God alone, and God cannot leave man alone.

God Is Forgiving

If the Christian is convinced of anything, he believes that he will be forgiven if he will turn from his selfish nature and let God reveal to him the wonders of his love. We have never given peace a chance on the earth. The mighty nations have not tried to deal with the less powerful nations on any other basis than that of exploitation. The fortunate groups have never wanted the less fortunate groups to share their rights and privileges. The man who occupies the vantage points has never been particularly eager to have his power threatened by another. But if man would repent in these areas and trust God, God would forgive him, and we would have a new heaven and a new earth.

As we attempt to improve race relations in America, we do it on the conviction that race prejudice can be eradicated and that discrimination can be abolished. We think this because of our belief that the nature of man can be improved. We know that we must not rely wholly on knowledge. We must have faith in God and trust him to bring us out all right even when we cannot see the end of our journey.

8.

belief in action

Jesus is the central figure and our guide for Christian living. But when anyone today is urged to accept Jesus, seldom is the fact taken into account that he is being advised to model his life after a man who was rejected by his generation and who was nailed to the cross between two thieves. The great majority of the members of the human race will never be willing to die for their convictions. Adults urge youth to do what most of those who are older have not done. We might as well be honest and admit that any person who attempts to live his or her life in accordance with the content of the life and teachings of Jesus is likely to find the going hard. It may not mean a physical death, but it may mean less social, economic, and political success.

Jesus Still Points the Way

Some people claim that Jesus lived in an age so different from ours that he has nothing to offer for our time. But we can reply that great truths, whether scientific or religious, are bounded neither by time nor by geography. For example, the definition of neighbor that Jesus gives in the story of the Good Samaritan will always be valid.

Jesus set forth certain fundamental principles for living that are applicable in our time and will no doubt be applicable in the ages to come. No Christian can deny the fact that the life and teachings of Jesus have important social implications. This is true, whether we move in the area of politics, industry, race, or international affairs.

Many of us are concerned about race. It is here that we are most likely to be shackled and bound by current practices, which we are afraid to break away from. Our Christian behavior breaks down perhaps more in this area than it does in any other. After the Christian faith has had its say about the unity of man in God and man's duty to man, and modern science has made its pronouncements as to the potential equality of the races, our customary behavior in the realm of race is likely to fall far below minimum Christian standards. We seem to lack the motivating power to act on what we say we believe about God, Jesus, and man, and similarly on what we say we believe about science. Our fears make cowards of us.

Our Fears Are Unfounded

We want to do what we believe or know is right but we fear the consequences. We fear we will lose our job, prestige, social standing, political or economic success. We say the time is not ripe. We believe the cause will be set back a quarter of a century if we change things. We fear there will be race riots and that race relations will be worse than they were before if we abolish segregation. So, instead of acting, we defend what is—even when we admit it is wrong. And yet experience proves that our greatest fears are usually fears of things that never happen.

73

In the last quarter of a century, great progress has been made in the area of race relations in the United States; more progress than in any comparable period since 1865. These examples will prove the point:

It was predicted by the timid and conservative that Southern white students would mob Negro students if they matriculated in Southern universities. They are there, and with a very few exceptions white Southern students have received them without incident.

Throughout the nation educational opportunities are being rapidly equalized. In many areas Negro teachers receive the same salaries as white teachers.

Discrimination in boxing and big league baseball is just about a thing of the past. It was predicted that white players would not play with Negroes. There wasn't a word of truth in it.

It was argued that if the armed forces were desegregated, white soldiers would not stand for it. The Army, Navy, Marine Corps, and Air Force are all desegregated, and white servicemen do not complain. It was predicted that it would never do to abolish segregation in the dining car and in interstate travel. Some predicted that there would be clashes between Negro and white passengers. There wasn't a word of truth in that either. Segregation in interstate travel and in the dining car is history, and there have been no clashes.

The South was fearful when the white primary was abolished. Again some people expected riots. There were none. Several Northern states have enacted civil rights legislation. And where state authorities and local school boards have accepted the responsibility of implementing the 1954 decision of the Supreme Court declaring segregation in the public schools unconstitutional, desegregation has gone forward in many places without serious conflict. It is mainly the resistance of politicians that has made some people rebellious and retarded the progress of desegregating the schools. As a rule, when the right forward step is taken after thoughtful preparation, the people will accept it and in the end be glad.

I was happy to recite these gains when I was in India in 1953. But I was not so happy when the people of India asked me how these gains had come about. I had to tell them that most of the progress resulted from coercive court action and that Negroes had to sue in the Federal courts to get what rightfully belongs to them under the Constitution of the United States. In some areas the churches took an active part in bringing about these accomplishments, especially in getting civil rights legislation, including fair employment practice laws.

Belief and Action Are Not in Conflict

Contrary to popular opinion, there is no conflict between belief and action. Beliefs are not theoretical ideas divorced from doing something. Beliefs always find expression in action. There may be a gulf between intellectual assent—merely agreeing that something is so—and action, but there is no gulf between really believing in something and acting upon it. It is psychologically impossible for one really to believe something and to act constantly contrary to that belief. It may be possible to have a temporary conflict between what we believe and what we do, but the conflict will eventually disappear. Our actual beliefs will soon be found to coincide with what we do.

Good educators never divorce theory from practice. Facts learned in physics and chemistry text books are tested in the laboratory. The study of mathematics and social sciences is supplemented by field work. Leaders in education plan demonstration classes where young teachers gain experience. The aspiring physician goes from medical school to an internship in which medical theory is reinforced and modified by the experiences of medical practice.

Knowledge is never ours until we have acted on it. It might be said that we know only that which we have experienced and our beliefs are confirmed only in actions. Beliefs are more than intellectual assents; they involve convictions, and convictions involve action. We believe what we do, and we are what we do.

If we say we believe in democracy and deny it to Jews, Mexicans, Japanese, Roman Catholics, labor or management, Negroes, or any others, we do not really believe in democracy.

If we say we believe that the life of each individual is of intrinsic value and is sacred unto God and if at the same time seek to exploit the individual and to take advantage of him, we do not believe in his intrinsic worth.

If we say that we believe in justice for all people, irrespective of race, and proceed to segregate, deny the ballot to, deny jobs to, and discriminate educationally against certain groups in the population on the grounds of race, we do not really believe in justice.

If we say we believe that every American should have equality of opportunity to develop his mind and character and do not work toward that end, we do not believe what we say.

The great pronouncements of the Christian religion on race and the great findings of modern science about race must somehow be acted upon by individuals who believe them before they can make any difference in real life.

The Responsible Self

It is true that one may be forced into doing things in which he does not believe, such as going to war and killing. One may find himself in an environment where it is suicidal to go against current practices or where heavy penalties are imposed if the law is broken. But even in such cases as these, one must find ways of keeping alive his beliefs through action or he may accept his environment and lose his beliefs.

A person who does not believe in segregation of the races but lives in a community where segregation is prescribed by law must find ways to have fellowship with those of other racial groups despite the law. He must act on his belief in Christian fellowship or he will cease to believe it. And the true Christian will always find ways to act. There are no known laws requiring churches to segregate races in their worship and membership. Here is an opportunity for the true Christian to act on his belief in Christian fellowship. A true Christian who believes in the fatherhood of God, the lordship of Jesus Christ, the brotherhood of man, and the dignity of every person and who believes that the church is God's house cannot deny fellowship in worship to another Christian nor deny membership to one of the same faith. If Islam can admit all races to the mosque and if atheistic communism can embrace all races in its fellowship without segregation, certainly the Christian can do the same in his church, and it is wholly within his power to do so. The Christian can also do his share to get laws of segregation repealed and decisions of the Supreme Court obeyed. Literally thousands of discriminatory laws have been enacted against Negroes, Mexicans, Orientals, and Indian Americans.

It matters not how unyielding the social pattern, how unbending the law, how terrible the possible social ostracism, the Christian who really believes in God and man will do something about his beliefs. He will recognize what so few people seem to see—that there is an area in every man's life, however small, over which he has complete control.

The ambulance driver in South Carolina who refused to carry an injured woman to a hospital solely because she was a Negro stood then and there in the presence of God and was responsible only to God. It did not matter what the current practices were. A human being had been struck by a car and was suffering. A higher loyalty than that to his company and community called that driver to duty. It was wholly within his power to help a dying woman, a child of God. A Christian would have responded to the will of God.

In a case like that, a Christian never would debate the question, "What will happen to my job?" He would obey God and trust him for results.

If the Christian will act in those areas where he has complete control, his power to act will grow and he will be able to act on his beliefs in more dangerous zones.

Even in areas where the Christian does not have complete control, he can act on his beliefs. The man who owns a business can do a great deal by setting up a policy of hiring and promoting people on the basis of character and competence, never on the basis of race. Throughout the centuries men devoted to a higher loyalty have risen above their environment and have helped to transform it. Man does not have to be a slave to his environment.

Faith in Action Leads to Brotherhood

This study began with God because he is the power behind the universe and man and because we reach our highest appreciation for man only when we recognize our kinship with man in God. The basic issues of life are not political nor economic. They are religious—God, man, ethics, and spiritual values. A belief in God and in man as revealed by Jesus is the most important issue facing the world today. If we could ever get the proper attitude toward God and man, we could more easily settle our political, economic, and social questions. I am talking about a belief in God that expresses itself in action. The true Christian not only has faith that leads to action, but he has faith that ultimately the results of his action will be good.

The most unfortunate thing about many so-called Christian people is that they proclaim their belief in God and straightway begin to act as if they did not believe in him. Many of us will take few risks because we do not trust God enough. We are afraid of the consequences of our actions. We want to know in advance what will happen to us if we do this or say that. Too many of us allow fear rather than faith to direct our conduct.

I do not mean to imply that the Christian will ask no questions in his approach to social problems. I mean to say that the Christian should be less cautious than the non-Christian, once he is assured of the right action to be taken, because he believes that the ultimate outcome of what he does is in the hands of God. Unless the Christian can have this kind of faith in God, it is difficult to see how he can act at all in the midst of fears and a hostile environment.

It would be surprising to know how few people would lose their jobs, positions, prestige, or popularity by taking a courageous stand or acting on beliefs and convictions that they know are right. And even if they should, it often takes a lifetime, and sometimes generations, to determine success or failure. All is not lost if temporarily we seem defeated. One of the deepest facts of spiritual experience lies in the ultimate success of apparent defeat. The greatest fears are frequently fears of things that never happen. The true Christian will act on his faith and trust God for the results.

Though not a professed Christian, Mahatma Gandhi had faith. He had faith in the ultimate triumph of that which is right. He believed that India should be free. He acted on the belief that love and nonviolence are stronger than hate and war. He went to jail for his beliefs and activities. But today India is free, and history will record that Mahatma Gandhi did more than any other one person to achieve independence for his people. He believed that fifty million untouchables should be able to walk the earth with dignity and live as human beings. He smashed customs and traditions and cast his lot with the depressed millions of India. He died of an assassin's bullet. But the things he lived for and died for have come to pass. Untouchability has been outlawed in India.

About a century ago Susan B. Anthony was almost mobbed because she believed that women should be educated on an equal basis with men and that they should have the right to vote. In 1872 she was arrested and fined because she voted in a November election. What she fought and lived for is here. Women are being educated without limitation, and they vote in every election.

Paul believed that Jesus Christ superseded the law, that in Christ "There is neither Jew nor Greek, there is neither slave nor free, there is neither male nor female; for you are all one in Christ Jesus" *Galatians* 3:28. Acting on this conviction and others, he suffered and died for the Christian cause. And yet Christianity's spread in history and in the world owes more to Paul than to any other individual.

Jesus had such faith. There can hardly be any doubting the fact that after nineteen long centuries, he is the one sure guide to salvation in this world and in the next. He points the way that leads men to brotherhood and nations to world peace.

questions for consideration and discussion

Chapter 1

1. Many non-Christian nations have accepted the Universal Declaration of Human Rights of the United Nations, and they do not divide their peoples according to race. Many local Christian churches, on the other hand, receive into membership persons of only one race. How can this difference in practice be accounted for?

2. What are some of the ways in which today we, in effect, call some people "common" or "unclean" (*Acts* 10:28)? Why do we do this?

3. What is the difference between being "decent" and being "Christian"? Relate your answer to the "statement about God" constituting this chapter.

Chapter 2

1. Study Paul's address to the Athenians in *Acts* 17:16-31. What ideas gained from this passage support the most important statements in this chapter?

2. List the ways in which science and religion agree on the origin, status, and kinship of men. Discuss any areas of disagreement that occur to you.

3. If a young person has been thoroughly saturated with prejudice by his family and society, is it really true that "with

God's help and grace, [he] can rise above prejudice against any religious or racial group"? If so, how?

Chapter 3

1. What are some of the difficult situations Christians face when they endeavor to act upon the principle that love of God and love of man are inseparable?

2. On the basis of the interpretation of a neighbor in the story of the Good Samaritan, who would be considered our neighbors today? Why?

3. List ways in which churches or Christians have demonstrated love for God as expressed through love for man.

Chapter 4

1. What is the basis for membership in our own local church? In other churches in our community?

2. Discuss the statement: "There is no limit to what the religious man must do to perfect reconciliation or right relationship with his fellow man."

3. From the Bible passages cited in this chapter, draw up a list of guiding principles showing how Christianity may strive "to perfect reconciliation."

Chapter 5

1. What does prejudice do to the person who practices discrimination? To the one who is the victim of discrimination?

2. Why are the attitudes and actions of the United States regarding race a matter of world significance?

3. What evidences can you give that the United States does have "untouchables" today?

Chapter 6

1. In what sense is the church that practices segregation more blameworthy than a business doing the same thing?

2. What is the official pronouncement of our denomination regarding race? Of other denominations? How do the practices of our local churches measure up to these pronouncements?

3. What should Christians do about laws that violate Christian principles?

Chapter 7

1. In what ways is unchanged human nature at the root of the problem centering around race? Why is this true?

2. If it is true that "knowledge does not insure goodness" and resolve racial difficulties, how can we hope for better relationships among races? What can be done?

3. What does the statement that once a person "allows God to come into his life, he is no longer a slave to the practices around him" mean for us today? What implications does it have for daily actions?

Chapter 8

1. Cite some instances in our own community that bear out the statement that "our fears make cowards of us"? What more helpful action could have been taken in these situations?

2. Describe the acts of some persons you have known or read about who have been able to act contrary to current racial practices in their communities? How do you feel about their actions?

3. What are four or five ways in which we can begin to act upon Paul's statement that Christians "are all one in Christ Jesus"?

The text of this book was set in linotype Times Roman, a type face created in 1932 by Stanley Morison, typographic consultant of The Monotype Corporation, Limited, for *The Times* (London). It was cut simultaneously by the English Monotype and Linotype companies as an interchangeable face. Although it was originally designed for periodical work, it has rapidly become very popular in all typographic fields because of its good color, legible design, economy of space, and excellent reproducing qualities.

COMPOSITION AND PRINTING BY SOWERS PRINTING COMPANY
COVERS AND JACKETS BY AFFILIATED LITHOGRAPHERS
BINDING BY BOOK CRAFTSMEN ASSOCIATES
FORMAT DESIGNED BY DOROTHY PAPY
BINDING DESIGNED BY LOUISE E. JEFFERSON